Change the Way People Perceive You

Unlocking the Secrets of Influence, Confidence, and Charisma

Tom Crowe

Copyright © <2025> <Tom Crowe>

Made with ❤ on the Notion Press Platform

www.notionpress.com

Contents

Foreword

Perception shapes reality. The way people see you—whether in the workplace, in social circles, or even in fleeting interactions—can determine your opportunities, influence, and success. But what if you had the power to shape that perception intentionally?

Change the Way People Perceive You is more than just a book; it's a **blueprint for mastering influence, exuding confidence, and unlocking the charisma that sets leaders apart**. In a world where first impressions are formed in seconds and reputations can be made or broken in an instant, the ability to **present yourself authentically yet powerfully is a game-changer**.

Through years of experience, research, and real-world observations, the author has distilled the **psychological, behavioral, and strategic principles** behind how others see us. This book doesn't just explain **what influence is—it shows you how to build it**. From mastering the science of body language to refining verbal and non-verbal cues, from developing presence in high-stakes conversations to cultivating long-term credibility, every chapter is designed to give you practical tools that you can apply immediately.

Whether you're a professional looking to **advance in your career**, a leader seeking to **motivate and inspire**, or simply someone who wants to **navigate social dynamics with ease**, this book provides a **structured, step-by-step approach to becoming the most compelling version of yourself**.

Influence isn't reserved for the lucky few—it's a skill that can be developed, refined, and wielded effectively. By the time you finish reading, you won't just understand how people perceive you; you'll have the tools to shape and enhance that perception—**on your terms**.

Get ready to transform the way the world sees you.

Preface

Perception is a powerful force—it shapes our relationships, influences our success, and determines how we navigate the world. Yet, most of us go through life without ever fully understanding **how others perceive us** or how we can take control of that perception. This book was born from a simple realization: **the ability to influence how others see you is not just an advantage—it is a necessity**.

Throughout my career, I have witnessed firsthand how confidence, communication, and charisma can open doors that qualifications alone cannot. I have seen individuals with **average skill sets but extraordinary presence rise to leadership**, while equally talented people struggle to gain recognition simply because they failed to project their value.

This book is my attempt to **decode the art of influence**—to take the principles of psychology, communication, and human interaction and turn them into a practical guide that anyone can use. Whether you're an aspiring professional, a leader, or someone who simply wants to improve their personal and social interactions, the insights in this book will help you **enhance your confidence, refine your presence, and develop the kind of charisma that leaves a lasting impact**.

But this is not just another book about self-improvement. It is a **step-by-step guide** to mastering the small but powerful changes that can **redefine how people see you**. Through research, real-world examples, and actionable techniques, I will show you how to **take control of your personal brand, communicate with influence, and create an authentic yet powerful presence**.

The ability to shape perception is not a skill reserved for the naturally gifted—it is something you can **learn, practice, and master**. And by the end of this book, you will be equipped with the tools to **change the way people perceive you—on your terms**.

Acknowledgments

Writing this book has been a journey of exploration, learning, and personal growth, and I could not have completed it without the support, guidance, and encouragement of many people along the way.

First and foremost, I am deeply grateful to **my family**, whose unwavering support has been my foundation. Their belief in me, even during moments of self-doubt, has been a driving force behind this project. To my spouse, whose patience and encouragement never wavered, and to my friends who listened to my ideas and provided valuable feedback—thank you for always being there.

A special thank you to **my mentors and colleagues**, who have inspired me throughout my professional journey. Your insights into leadership, communication, and influence have profoundly shaped the principles in this book. Many of the lessons shared here are a result of the experiences and wisdom gained from working alongside brilliant minds.

I also want to express my gratitude to **my readers**—those who seek to grow, improve, and take control of the way they are perceived in the world. Your willingness to invest in yourself and your future is what makes this work meaningful. If even one person benefits from the insights in this book, then my effort has been worthwhile.

To the countless authors, researchers, and thought leaders whose work has contributed to my understanding of influence, confidence, and charisma—thank you for your contributions to the world of knowledge.

Lastly, I am thankful to everyone who encouraged me to put these thoughts into words. Writing a book is not a solitary endeavor, and I am fortunate to have had the support of so many incredible people.

This book is for all of you.

Prologue/Introduction

How do people see you? More importantly, how do you want them to see you?

Every interaction—whether in the workplace, at social gatherings, or even online—leaves an impression. Some people naturally command attention, while others struggle to be noticed. Some effortlessly gain respect and admiration, while others constantly feel overlooked. What makes the difference? **It's not just talent, intelligence, or luck—it's perception.**

The way others perceive you can open doors or close them. It can influence job opportunities, relationships, and even the way you see yourself. But here's the good news: **perception is not fixed—it can be shaped, refined, and transformed.**

This book is your **step-by-step guide to mastering the way people perceive you**. Whether you want to project confidence in meetings, establish authority in leadership, or build meaningful connections in social settings, the tools in this book will help you take control of your personal brand.

Throughout these pages, you'll discover:
The psychology of first impressions and how to make them work for you
How to communicate with confidence, even when you don't feel confident
The subtle but powerful signals that determine trust, influence, and authority
How to overcome self-doubt and imposter syndrome
Techniques to enhance your charisma and presence in any room

This isn't just another book on self-improvement. It's a practical guide, filled with actionable strategies you can apply immediately. You don't have to change who you are—you just need to **unlock the potential of how others see you**.

Are you ready to take control of the way the world perceives you? Let's get started.

Chapter 1: The Power of Perception

Perception is the lens through which others interpret your actions, words, and presence. It's not about who you *think* you are—it's about how others *see* you. From the moment you walk into a room, your posture, tone, and even the energy you radiate begin to tell a story about you. But here's the catch: the story others perceive isn't always the one you intend to tell.

Why Perception Matters

Every interaction in life is shaped by perception. Whether you're interviewing for a job, pitching an idea, or building a relationship, people base their decisions on their perception of you, often subconsciously. It's not just about what you do—it's about how you make people feel, how you communicate your intentions, and whether others see you as someone they can trust, respect, or follow.

Take this example: Imagine two equally qualified candidates walk into an interview. The first exudes confidence through clear speech, purposeful movements, and an engaging smile. The second avoids eye contact, speaks hesitantly, and fidgets nervously. Despite their identical qualifications, the first candidate leaves a stronger impression simply because of how they are *perceived*.

The truth is, perception can make or break opportunities, relationships, and careers. But here's the empowering part: perception isn't fixed—it can be *shaped*.

What Shapes Perception?

Perception is influenced by a variety of factors:

- **Appearance**: People form opinions based on how you present yourself physically—your grooming, attire, and overall style.

- **Body Language**: Nonverbal communication like posture, gestures, and facial expressions often speak louder than words.

- **Tone of Voice**: The way you say something can be as impactful as what you say. Warm, confident tones foster trust, while hesitant or aggressive tones can create distance.

- **Actions**: Your behavior—how you treat others, follow through on commitments, and handle adversity—forms the foundation of how people perceive your character.

By understanding these elements, you gain the power to influence and shape how others see you.

The Role of Self-Awareness

To change how others perceive you, you must first understand how you perceive yourself. Are you sending the signals you intend to send? Often, there's a gap between how we see ourselves and how others see us. Closing this gap starts with honest self-reflection and feedback from trusted sources.

Ask yourself:

- How do I come across in conversations?

- Do I seem approachable and confident, or distant and unsure?

- What do people say about me when I'm not in the room?

The answers to these questions will provide invaluable insight into your current personal brand—the perception you're already creating.

The Misconception About Being "Fake"

Many people resist the idea of shaping perception because they fear it means being inauthentic. But shaping perception isn't about pretending to be someone you're not—it's about aligning how others see you with who you truly are. If you're a kind, capable person, why not ensure that's what people notice first?

Think of it like this: If a gem isn't polished, its brilliance won't shine, no matter how valuable it is. Similarly, if you don't consciously manage the way you're perceived, people may never fully appreciate your true potential.

Real-Life Example: The Story of Abraham Lincoln

Abraham Lincoln is often remembered as one of history's most respected leaders, but early in his career, he wasn't always taken seriously. His lanky frame, rustic appearance, and self-taught background led many to underestimate him. Yet, Lincoln consciously reshaped how people perceived him by honing his public speaking skills, emphasizing his intelligence, and demonstrating empathy and humor. Over time, he turned these deliberate efforts into strengths that earned him the nickname "Honest Abe" and solidified his legacy.

What This Means for You

The way people perceive you is a reflection of your choices—your words, actions, and how you show up in the world. The good news? You have the power to change it, starting today. Whether you want to project confidence in meetings, build stronger relationships, or inspire others to follow your lead, small, intentional changes can make a big difference.

Action Steps to Start Shaping Perception Today

1. **Seek Feedback**: Ask a trusted friend or colleague how they perceive you. Focus on areas where your intentions and their perceptions don't align.

2. **Improve Your Body Language**: Stand tall, make eye contact, and use open gestures to appear more confident and approachable.

3. **Refine Your Appearance**: Dress in a way that aligns with the message you want to convey—whether it's professionalism, creativity, or reliability.

4. **Practice Empathy**: Show genuine interest in others by listening actively and validating their feelings. People perceive empathetic individuals as trustworthy and likable.

5. **Monitor Your Tone**: Pay attention to how you sound. Practice speaking clearly and with confidence, even in casual conversations.

Conclusion

Perception isn't destiny—it's a tool you can control. By understanding its power and taking deliberate steps to manage it, you can create a lasting impression that aligns with your true self. Remember, the world sees you as you present yourself. What story are you telling? Let's start shaping it, one interaction at a time.

Chapter 2: The Science Behind First Impressions

First impressions are formed faster than you might think—research shows that it takes just **seven seconds** for someone to form an opinion about you. Whether you're walking into a job interview, meeting a client, or even entering a social gathering, those initial moments are critical. But what exactly happens during those few seconds, and how can you take control of the narrative?

The Psychology of First Impressions

Humans are hardwired to make snap judgments. Psychologists call this phenomenon "thin-slicing," which refers to the brain's ability to draw conclusions based on limited information. In these moments, our subconscious minds analyze a variety of cues—your appearance, body language, facial expressions, tone of voice, and even the way you carry yourself.

Why does this happen?
In prehistoric times, survival often depended on quickly assessing whether someone was a friend or foe. While we no longer face predators in the wild, our brains still default to these rapid evaluations in social and professional settings.

What First Impressions Are Based On

The elements that shape first impressions include:

1. **Appearance**: People often judge your competence and trustworthiness based on how you're dressed and groomed.

2. **Body Language**: Open and confident postures convey approachability, while slouched or closed-off stances suggest insecurity or disinterest.

3. **Facial Expressions**: A warm smile can immediately make you seem likable, while a neutral or stern expression may come across as unapproachable.

4. **Tone of Voice**: The pitch, speed, and volume of your speech heavily influence how people perceive your confidence and credibility.

Studies reveal that **nonverbal cues** like body language and facial expressions make up more than 55% of how others perceive you during first encounters, while tone of voice contributes 38%. Only 7% of perception comes from the actual words you say during that initial interaction.

The "Halo Effect" and Its Impact

The first impression you make often creates a **halo effect**, where the initial opinion influences how someone views everything about you moving forward. For example:

- If you're perceived as confident in the first meeting, others are likely to assume you're competent and trustworthy as well.

- Conversely, if you come across as unsure or disengaged, you may need significant effort to overcome that perception later.

Real-Life Example: Steve Jobs' Reinvention

In the early stages of his career, Steve Jobs was often criticized for being abrasive and unpolished. However, when he returned to Apple in the late 1990s, he consciously reinvented his image. From his signature black turtleneck to his polished presentation skills, Jobs crafted a first impression that exuded innovation, focus, and leadership. His transformation demonstrated that first impressions aren't permanent—they can be intentionally reshaped to align with your goals.

The Role of Cultural and Contextual Factors

First impressions are not universal; they are shaped by cultural and contextual factors.

- In Western cultures, a firm handshake signals confidence, while in some Asian cultures, a respectful bow may convey humility and respect.

- Context matters, too. What works in a casual setting may not work in a formal business environment.

By understanding your audience and adjusting your approach accordingly, you can make first impressions that resonate.

Common First Impression Pitfalls to Avoid

1. **Over-Apologizing**: Apologizing excessively can make you seem unsure of yourself.

2. **Neglecting Appearance**: While it's tempting to downplay looks, dressing appropriately shows respect for the situation and yourself.

3. **Avoiding Eye Contact**: Failing to make eye contact can signal dishonesty or lack of confidence.

4. **Talking Too Much (or Too Little)**: Dominating the conversation can come across as self-centered, while being too quiet may seem disinterested.

How to Master First Impressions

1. Prepare Ahead:
Before any significant interaction, ask yourself: What message do I want to convey? Tailor your appearance, tone, and mindset to align with your goals.

2. Focus on Nonverbal Cues:

- Stand tall with shoulders back to project confidence.

- Smile genuinely to appear approachable and warm.

- Maintain steady, friendly eye contact.

3. Use a Confident Introduction:
Start with a firm handshake, a clear voice, and an introduction that highlights your role or purpose. Example: "Hi, I'm [Your Name]. I'm really excited to meet you and discuss [topic]."

4. Be Present and Engaged:
Show genuine interest by actively listening and responding thoughtfully. People are more likely to remember how you made them feel than what you said.

5. Mirror Positive Behaviors:
Subtly mirroring the other person's tone or gestures can create a sense of connection and trust.

Quick Fixes for Immediate Results

1. **Dress with Intention:** Choose outfits that match the occasion and project professionalism.

2. **Take a Power Pause:** Take a deep breath before entering a room to calm nerves and focus your energy.

3. **Speak with Purpose:** Avoid filler words like "um" and "like." Speak clearly and confidently.

4. **Practice Gratitude:** People are drawn to positivity. Start interactions with a compliment or thank you.

Conclusion

First impressions are formed in a flash, but their impact can last a lifetime. By understanding the science behind these snap judgments and taking deliberate steps to manage how others perceive you, you can set the tone for deeper trust, respect, and connection. Remember, every interaction is an opportunity to make a lasting impression—don't leave it to chance.

Chapter 3: The Transformative Power of Self-Awareness

How often do you stop to reflect on how others perceive you? The truth is, many of us live on autopilot, unaware of the signals we send out daily. But without self-awareness, it's impossible to shape how the world sees you. This chapter focuses on the transformative power of understanding yourself—your strengths, weaknesses, habits, and the impact you have on others.

What Is Self-Awareness?

Self-awareness is the ability to recognize and understand your own emotions, thoughts, and behaviors—and how they influence the people around you. It's the foundation for personal growth, allowing you to bridge the gap between how you *see yourself* and how others *perceive you*.

Imagine a coworker who thinks they're funny but constantly interrupts others with poorly timed jokes. While they see themselves as the office comedian, others may find them distracting. This disconnect often arises from a lack of self-awareness.

The Two Dimensions of Self-Awareness

1. **Internal Self-Awareness:** Understanding your emotions, motivations, and values.
   Example: Why do you get defensive during feedback? What drives your choices in tough situations?

2. **External Self-Awareness:** Understanding how others perceive you.

Example: Do your colleagues see you as a team player or someone who takes over conversations?

Both dimensions are critical for shaping perception and building meaningful connections.

Why Self-Awareness Is Transformative

When you understand yourself, you gain control over your behavior and can align your actions with your goals. Self-aware people:

- Communicate with clarity and purpose.

- Build stronger, more authentic relationships.

- Adapt to challenges without losing confidence.

Research shows that self-aware leaders are more effective, employees with high self-awareness are better collaborators, and individuals with greater self-insight experience higher personal satisfaction.

Real-Life Example: Oprah Winfrey's Self-Awareness Journey

Oprah Winfrey's rise to success wasn't just about talent—it was about deep self-awareness. Early in her career, Oprah realized that trying to emulate other television personalities didn't feel authentic. Instead, she leaned into her natural empathy and authenticity, transforming how audiences perceived her. By staying true to herself, she built a brand that resonates with millions worldwide.

How to Cultivate Self-Awareness

1. Seek Honest Feedback:

Ask trusted friends, colleagues, or mentors:

- "What's one thing I do well that stands out to you?"

- "What's one habit of mine that could use improvement?"

Hearing others' perspectives can reveal blind spots you might not recognize.

2. Reflect Daily:

At the end of each day, ask yourself:

- "What went well today, and why?"

- "What could I have done differently?"
  Journaling these reflections helps identify patterns in your behavior.

3. Monitor Your Emotions:

Pay attention to how you react to different situations. For example:

- Do you shut down when receiving criticism?

- Do you dominate conversations when you feel nervous?
  Understanding emotional triggers allows you to respond more intentionally.

4. Observe Your Impact on Others:

Notice how people respond to your actions and words. Do they seem engaged, distant, or confused? Their reactions often mirror the signals you're sending.

5. Take Personality Assessments:

Tools like the **MBTI (Myers-Briggs)** or **DISC** profile can offer insights into your personality, strengths, and behavioral tendencies.

Common Barriers to Self-Awareness

1. **Defensiveness:** Rejecting feedback because it feels uncomfortable.

2. **Overconfidence:** Believing you're already self-aware and dismissing others' perceptions.

3. **Fear of Introspection:** Avoiding self-reflection because it might reveal uncomfortable truths.

These barriers can keep you stuck in patterns that negatively influence how others see you. Overcoming them requires courage and humility.

The Ripple Effect of Self-Awareness

When you're self-aware, you naturally project confidence and authenticity. People are drawn to those who seem genuine and in control of their emotions. As a result:

- Your relationships become stronger because others trust and respect you.

- You're more effective in professional settings because you understand how to adapt to different audiences.

- You experience personal growth as you align your behavior with your values and goals.

Quick Exercises to Build Self-Awareness Today

1. **Mirror Check:** Before important interactions, look in the mirror and assess your body language. Do you look confident and approachable?

2. **Pause and Observe:** During conversations, pause for a moment to observe how others are reacting. Are they engaged or disengaged? Adjust as needed.

3. **The 3-Word Exercise:** Ask three people to describe you in three words. Compare their answers with how you'd describe yourself. The gaps may reveal areas for growth.

Conclusion

Self-awareness is the key to unlocking your full potential. By understanding who you are and how others perceive you, you gain the ability to shape your personal narrative with intention. Like a sculptor chiseling away at a block of marble, the more self-aware you become, the more clearly your true self emerges. The result? A version of you that others see as authentic, confident, and inspiring.

This journey begins with one question: *How well do you know yourself?*

Chapter 4: Lessons from History's Game-Changers

Throughout history, there have been individuals who redefined how the world saw them. They transformed challenges into opportunities and reshaped perceptions with deliberate actions. What can we learn from them? This chapter dives into powerful examples of historical figures who mastered the art of perception and how their lessons apply to your life.

Reinvention Through Resilience: Abraham Lincoln

When Abraham Lincoln first entered politics, he was underestimated due to his humble background, awkward appearance, and lack of formal education. Yet, Lincoln turned these perceived weaknesses into strengths. He built a reputation for honesty, empathy, and integrity. By aligning his actions with his core values, Lincoln became one of the most respected leaders in history.

Key Takeaway: Consistency in values and actions builds trust and changes how people perceive you over time.

Charisma and Vision: Martin Luther King Jr.

Martin Luther King Jr. wasn't just a civil rights leader—he was a master of influence. His ability to inspire was rooted in his powerful speeches, empathetic connection with people, and unshakable belief in his vision. King's "I Have a Dream" speech remains a timeless example of how clear communication can inspire hope and action.

Key Takeaway: A strong vision paired with confident communication can make you unforgettable.

The Power of Authenticity: Oprah Winfrey

Oprah Winfrey started her career facing criticism for not fitting the traditional mold of a television personality. Instead of conforming, she embraced her authenticity—connecting with audiences on an emotional level. Her empathetic interviewing style and genuine nature built a global brand of trust and relatability.

Key Takeaway: Authenticity resonates deeply. Being true to yourself can set you apart in any field.

Overcoming Stigma: Malala Yousafzai

After surviving an attack for advocating girls' education, Malala Yousafzai became a global symbol of courage and resilience. Despite her young age, she used her voice to challenge oppressive systems and inspire millions. Her Nobel Peace Prize win solidified her as a leader in advocating for change.

Key Takeaway: Turning adversity into advocacy can reshape how the world sees you and amplify your impact.

Rewriting the Rules: Steve Jobs

Steve Jobs transformed his career trajectory by focusing on vision, innovation, and presentation. Known for his perfectionism, he refined not only the products Apple delivered but also his public image. His black turtleneck became a symbol of simplicity and innovation, reflecting his brand.

Key Takeaway: Attention to detail in how you present yourself and your work can leave a lasting impression.

How You Can Apply These Lessons

1. **Turn Weaknesses into Strengths:**
   Like Lincoln, reflect on traits others may underestimate and think about how to reframe them as strengths. For instance, humility can be seen as approachability, and inexperience can signal a fresh perspective.

2. **Build a Strong Vision:**
   Learn from Martin Luther King Jr.—clarify what you stand for and communicate it effectively. When people see you as a visionary, they're more likely to follow and support you.

3. **Be Authentic:**
   As Oprah proved, there's no substitute for being genuine. Stop trying to fit into molds that don't reflect your true self, and focus on building connections through authenticity.

4. **Use Adversity to Empower Yourself:**
   Malala's story reminds us that challenges don't define us—our response to them does. Use difficult experiences as a platform to showcase your resilience and purpose.

5. **Own Your Presentation:**
   Like Steve Jobs, ensure that how you present yourself, whether in person, through work, or online, reflects your desired image. Details matter, from your clothing to your email signature.

Exercises to Apply Historical Lessons

- **Personal Brand Statement:** Write a one-sentence statement that encapsulates your values and what you stand for. This

helps clarify how you want others to see you.
Example: "I'm someone who brings innovative solutions while fostering collaboration."

- **Reframe a Perceived Weakness:** Identify one trait you think is holding you back and reframe it into a positive.
Example: If you're shy, think of it as being thoughtful and reflective.

- **Envision Your Ideal Self:** Picture yourself in five years. How do you want people to describe you? List three qualities and start embodying them now.

Conclusion

History's most influential figures weren't born with universal admiration—they earned it by reshaping perceptions and aligning their actions with their vision. Whether you're navigating challenges or striving for new opportunities, their stories prove that it's never too late to redefine how the world sees you.

Ask yourself: *What story am I telling, and how can I rewrite it to reflect the person I want to become?*

Chapter 5: The Art of Nonverbal Communication

They say actions speak louder than words, and nowhere is this truer than in the realm of nonverbal communication. Studies suggest that up to **93% of communication** is nonverbal, relying on body language, facial expressions, and tone of voice to convey meaning. Whether you realize it or not, every movement you make, every expression you wear, and every gesture you use sends a message to those around you. In this chapter, we'll explore how to master nonverbal communication to project confidence, authenticity, and trust.

The Science of Nonverbal Communication

Nonverbal cues are processed instinctively by the brain, often faster than verbal communication. This means people form opinions about your intentions and emotions based on these signals before you even speak.

The key elements of nonverbal communication include:

1. **Body Language**: Your posture, gestures, and physical movements.

2. **Facial Expressions**: Smiles, frowns, raised eyebrows—all of these convey emotion instantly.

3. **Eye Contact**: Signals trust, attention, and confidence.

4. **Tone of Voice**: The pitch, volume, and pace of your speech can completely change the meaning of your words.

Why Nonverbal Communication Matters

Imagine meeting someone who says, "I'm really excited to be here," but their arms are crossed, their shoulders are slouched, and they avoid eye contact. Would you believe them? Probably not. This disconnect between words and nonverbal cues creates mistrust and confusion.

When your nonverbal communication aligns with your verbal message, it creates clarity, builds rapport, and enhances your credibility.

Mastering Body Language

1. Posture:
Your posture communicates your energy and confidence.

- **Confident posture**: Stand tall with your shoulders back, head held high, and feet firmly planted. This signals self-assurance.

- **Avoid**: Slouching or leaning excessively, which can make you appear disengaged or unsure.

2. Gestures:

- Use open and purposeful gestures to emphasize your points. For example, subtle hand movements can make your communication more engaging.

- Avoid fidgeting, pointing, or crossing your arms, as these can signal nervousness or defensiveness.

3. Movement:

- Move with intention. Walking confidently into a room or standing firmly during a conversation conveys authority.

The Importance of Eye Contact

Eye contact is one of the most powerful tools in nonverbal communication. It builds trust and shows that you are engaged and confident.

- Aim to maintain eye contact **70-80% of the time** during a conversation.

- Avoid staring, which can feel intimidating, or looking away frequently, which can signal discomfort or lack of interest.

Facial Expressions: Your Emotional Mirror

Your face often betrays your emotions, even when you don't say a word.

- A genuine smile can make you appear approachable and likable.

- Neutral or stern expressions may unintentionally make you seem distant or unwelcoming.

- Practice being mindful of your resting face—does it communicate openness, or does it unintentionally send the wrong signal?

Tone of Voice: The Hidden Message

The way you speak often carries more weight than the words you use.

- A calm and steady tone conveys confidence.

- Variations in pitch and emphasis can make you sound more dynamic and engaging.

- Avoid speaking too fast, as it can signal nervousness, or too slowly, as it may seem disinterested.

Real-Life Example: Barack Obama's Nonverbal Mastery

Barack Obama's public speaking success is not just about his words—it's about how he delivers them. His steady eye contact, open gestures, and calm tone of voice project confidence and credibility. Even in high-pressure situations, his controlled body language reassures and connects with audiences, making him one of the most effective communicators of his time.

How to Improve Your Nonverbal Communication

1. **Record Yourself:**
   Film yourself during a conversation or presentation. Pay attention to your posture, gestures, and tone of voice. Identify areas for improvement.

2. **Practice in the Mirror:**
   Observe your facial expressions while speaking. Do they align with your intended emotions?

3. **Adopt a Power Pose:**
   Before important interactions, try a power pose (e.g., standing tall with arms on your hips). Research shows that adopting powerful postures can boost confidence.

4. **Seek Feedback:**
   Ask trusted friends or colleagues for honest feedback on your nonverbal communication.

5. **Observe Others:**
   Watch videos of effective speakers or leaders. Notice how they use body language and tone to enhance their message.

Common Mistakes to Avoid

1. **Mixed Signals**: Saying one thing but your body language says another (e.g., saying "I'm fine" while avoiding eye contact).

2. **Excessive Gestures**: Overusing hand movements can distract from your message.

3. **Poor Posture**: Slouching or fidgeting makes you seem unconfident.

4. **Weak Handshakes**: A limp handshake can leave a negative impression—practice a firm, confident grip.

Quick Nonverbal Hacks to Try Today

- **Smile more**: A genuine smile instantly makes you more approachable.

- **Stand tall**: Check your posture when entering a room—it sets the tone for how others perceive you.

- **Pause and breathe**: Slowing down your speech and movements conveys calmness and control.

- **Mirror others**: Subtly mirroring the body language of those you're speaking with creates a sense of connection.

Conclusion

Nonverbal communication is the silent force shaping how others perceive you. By mastering your body language, tone of voice, and facial expressions, you can project confidence, authenticity, and trust.

Remember, every gesture, glance, and movement tells a story—make sure it's the one you want others to hear.

What does your body language say about you today?

Chapter 6: Rewriting Your Personal Brand

Your personal brand is the story people tell about you when you're not in the room. It's the impression you leave behind in the minds of colleagues, friends, clients, and even strangers. But here's the good news: your personal brand is not fixed—it's a dynamic, evolving narrative that you can intentionally shape and rewrite.

This chapter will guide you through understanding, defining, and enhancing your personal brand to align with the way you want to be perceived.

What Is a Personal Brand?

A personal brand is a combination of your skills, values, personality, and the way you present yourself to the world. It's not just your job title or social media presence—it's the total package of how others experience you.

Example: Think of Elon Musk. His personal brand conveys innovation, ambition, and a touch of eccentricity. Whether you agree with him or not, his brand is instantly recognizable and consistent across everything he does.

Why Your Personal Brand Matters

Your personal brand can open doors or close them. It influences:

- **Opportunities:** Employers, clients, and collaborators look for people who align with their values and goals.

- **Trust:** A strong, consistent brand builds trust and credibility.

- **Influence:** A clear brand makes you memorable and helps you stand out in competitive environments.

Signs Your Personal Brand Needs a Rewrite

- People often misunderstand your intentions or skills.

- You're overlooked for opportunities or promotions.

- You struggle to communicate your unique value.

- Your online presence doesn't reflect your real-life personality or goals.

If any of these sound familiar, it's time to take control and rewrite your narrative.

Steps to Define and Rewrite Your Personal Brand

1. Identify Your Core Values

Your personal brand should reflect your values, as they form the foundation of trust and authenticity.

- Ask yourself: What do I stand for? What matters most to me?

- Examples: Integrity, creativity, leadership, empathy, or resilience.

2. Define Your Unique Value Proposition (UVP)

Your UVP is what sets you apart from others.

- Ask yourself: What do I do better than most people? What problems can I solve?

- Example: "I'm a problem-solver who thrives under pressure and helps teams achieve their goals efficiently."

3. Audit Your Current Brand

Take stock of how you're currently perceived.

- Seek feedback: Ask colleagues, friends, or mentors how they would describe you.

- Review your online presence: Does your social media or LinkedIn profile reflect the professional and personal image you want to convey?

4. Craft Your Brand Statement

Summarize who you are, what you do, and why it matters in one clear sentence.

- Example: "I'm a results-driven leader who empowers teams to excel by fostering collaboration and innovation."

5. Align Your Actions with Your Brand

Your brand isn't just what you say—it's what you do. Make sure your actions, communication, and behavior consistently reflect your brand.

6. Build a Strong Online Presence

In today's world, your digital footprint is an extension of your personal brand.

- Update your LinkedIn profile with a professional photo, a compelling headline, and a summary that highlights your UVP.

- Share content that aligns with your expertise or values (e.g., articles, insights, or achievements).

Real-Life Example: Michelle Obama's Authentic Brand

Michelle Obama's personal brand is built on authenticity, grace, and advocacy. From her role as First Lady to her work as an author and speaker, she consistently communicates her values of family, education, and empowerment. Her book, *Becoming*, gave readers a deeper glimpse into her story, further reinforcing her brand as relatable and inspiring.

Key Takeaway: Authenticity and consistency are the cornerstones of a strong personal brand.

Pitfalls to Avoid While Shaping Your Brand

1. **Inauthenticity:** Trying to be someone you're not is unsustainable and easily detected by others.

2. **Inconsistency:** A personal brand that shifts too often can confuse people.

3. **Neglecting Your Online Presence:** Failing to curate your digital footprint can leave a gap between how you're perceived online and in real life.

Practical Tips to Strengthen Your Brand

1. **Network Intentionally:** Surround yourself with people who align with your goals and values.

2. **Be a Lifelong Learner:** Continuously develop skills that align with your brand and showcase this growth.

3. **Communicate Your Story:** Share your journey, challenges, and achievements to connect with others on a deeper level.

Quick Exercises to Strengthen Your Personal Brand Today

- **Define Your Legacy:** Write down how you want people to describe you 10 years from now.

- **Craft a 30-Second Introduction:** Prepare a short pitch about who you are and what you do, highlighting your UVP.

- **Audit Your Social Media:** Review your profiles and remove any content that doesn't align with your brand.

Conclusion

Rewriting your personal brand is not about changing who you are—it's about intentionally showcasing your best self to the world. By aligning your values, skills, and actions with the way you want to be perceived, you can create a brand that opens doors, builds trust, and leaves a lasting impression.

Ask yourself: *What story am I telling, and is it the one I want others to hear?* The power to rewrite it is in your hands.

Chapter 7: The Mirror Effect: Shaping Perception Through Empathy

Empathy is one of the most powerful tools for reshaping how others perceive you. When you genuinely understand and connect with people on an emotional level, it fosters trust, respect, and likability. This chapter explores how the mirror effect—where people reflect the energy and emotions they sense from you—can be a game-changer in your relationships and reputation.

What Is the Mirror Effect?

The mirror effect is a psychological phenomenon where people tend to reflect the emotions, attitudes, and behaviors of those around them. If you project positivity, confidence, and understanding, others are more likely to respond in kind. Conversely, negativity or indifference often leads to disengagement or mistrust.

Example: Think of a leader who listens attentively and validates their team's concerns versus one who dismisses or ignores them. The former inspires loyalty, while the latter creates resentment.

Why Empathy Matters in Shaping Perception

Empathy—the ability to understand and share the feelings of others—is the cornerstone of meaningful human connections. When people feel seen, heard, and valued, they're more likely to see you as trustworthy, compassionate, and relatable.

Research shows that empathy enhances leadership, improves workplace relationships, and even strengthens personal bonds. Empathetic individuals are often perceived as approachable and likable, traits that can significantly enhance how others view you.

How Empathy Shapes Perception

1. **Builds Trust:**
   When you actively listen and respond with understanding, people feel safe and respected, which fosters trust.

2. **Improves Communication:**
   Empathy helps you tailor your communication to the needs and emotions of others, making your message more impactful.

3. **Defuses Conflict:**
   Understanding the other person's perspective can help resolve disagreements more effectively and maintain positive relationships.

4. **Strengthens Influence:**
   People are more likely to follow or support someone who shows genuine care for their well-being.

Empathy in Action: Real-Life Examples

1. Nelson Mandela's Empathy-Driven Leadership:
Despite spending 27 years in prison, Nelson Mandela emerged as a leader who empathized with both his followers and his former oppressors. By understanding the fears and needs of all sides, he united a divided nation and earned global respect.

Key Takeaway: Empathy doesn't mean agreeing with everyone—it means seeking to understand and address their underlying concerns.

2. Howard Schultz and Starbucks:
When Starbucks CEO Howard Schultz faced financial challenges, he prioritized listening to employees and customers. His empathetic leadership helped restore trust in the company and turned it into a global powerhouse.

Key Takeaway: Empathy in business isn't just about kindness—it's a strategy for building strong, lasting relationships.

How to Develop Empathy

1. Practice Active Listening:

- Pay full attention to the person speaking without interrupting.

- Summarize what they said to show you've understood their perspective.

- Use phrases like, "I hear you" or "That must have been difficult for you."

2. Put Yourself in Their Shoes:

- Imagine what the other person might be feeling or thinking based on their situation.

- Ask questions to clarify their perspective, such as, "Can you help me understand how this affects you?"

3. Be Curious, Not Judgmental:

- Approach conversations with curiosity rather than forming immediate conclusions.

- Replace "Why did you do that?" with "What led you to that decision?"

4. Observe Nonverbal Cues:

- Pay attention to body language, facial expressions, and tone of voice to gain deeper insight into how someone feels.

5. Show Appreciation and Validation:

- Acknowledge others' emotions and efforts, even if you don't fully agree with their views.

- Example: "I can see how much effort you've put into this, and I appreciate it."

The Ripple Effect of Empathy

When you approach people with empathy, they're likely to mirror that behavior. This ripple effect can transform relationships, foster collaboration, and enhance your overall reputation. Empathy not only reshapes how others perceive you but also creates a positive environment around you.

Practical Exercises to Build Empathy Today

1. **The 5-Minute Rule:**
   Spend five uninterrupted minutes each day listening to someone without offering solutions—just focus on understanding their perspective.

2. **Empathy Journaling:**
   Reflect on a recent interaction where you felt misunderstood. Write down how the other person might have perceived the situation.

3. **Ask, Don't Assume:**
   In your next conversation, ask at least one open-ended question to learn more about the other person's feelings or experiences.

4. **Mirror Emotions:**

   Practice subtly mirroring the emotions and tone of the person you're speaking with to create a sense of connection.

Common Mistakes to Avoid

1. **Faking Empathy:** Pretending to care is easily detected and can damage trust. Be genuine in your approach.

2. **Over-Sympathizing:** Empathy is about understanding, not pity. Avoid responses that make others feel powerless or pitied.

3. **Assuming You Know:** Don't project your feelings onto someone else; instead, ask questions to clarify their perspective.

Quick Wins to Apply Empathy in Daily Life

- Start meetings by asking how people are feeling or what's on their mind.

- Pause before responding in conflicts and consider the other person's point of view.

- Offer small acts of kindness, like acknowledging a coworker's effort or checking in on a friend.

Conclusion

Empathy is the bridge that connects you to others on a deeper level. By understanding their needs, feelings, and perspectives, you can reshape how they see you—as a compassionate, trustworthy, and influential individual.

In the words of Maya Angelou: *"People will forget what you said, people will forget what you did, but people will never forget how you made them feel."* Let empathy be the key to leaving a lasting positive impression.

Chapter 8: Mastering the Art of Communication

Communication is the backbone of every relationship, opportunity, and success. It's not just about the words you say—it's about how you say them, when you say them, and the intention behind them. Mastering communication is about delivering your message with clarity, confidence, and connection. This chapter focuses on how to refine your communication skills to shape how others perceive you in every interaction.

The True Power of Communication

Think about the most inspiring leaders, charismatic speakers, or trusted mentors in your life. What sets them apart? Chances are, it's their ability to communicate ideas in ways that resonate with others. Great communicators don't just share information—they influence, inspire, and build trust.

Example: Imagine a manager giving feedback. One says, "You made a mistake; you need to fix this." The other says, "Here's what went wrong, but I see this as an opportunity for you to grow. Let's work on it together." Both deliver the same core message, but the second approach fosters understanding and motivation.

Elements of Effective Communication

1. **Clarity:** Ensure your message is simple, clear, and easy to understand. Avoid jargon or ambiguity.

2. **Empathy:** Tailor your message to your audience's needs, feelings, and perspectives.

3. **Confidence:** Speak with assurance to build credibility and trust.

4. **Authenticity:** Be genuine in your tone and content—people can sense when you're not being real.

5. **Active Listening:** Communication isn't just about speaking; it's about truly hearing and understanding the other person.

Verbal Communication: Say It Right

1. The Power of Tone:

- A warm, steady tone builds trust and connection.

- Avoid monotony or harshness, which can disengage or intimidate your audience.

2. Choose Your Words Wisely:

- Use positive, empowering language.
  Example: Replace "I can't" with "Let's find a way."

- Avoid overusing filler words like "um," "like," or "you know."

3. Pause for Impact:

- Strategic pauses can emphasize key points and make your words more powerful.

4. Be Concise:

- Say more with fewer words. Long-winded explanations can dilute your message.

Nonverbal Communication: Show It Right

1. Body Language:

- Maintain open postures—no crossed arms or slouching.

- Use purposeful gestures to support your words, but avoid overdoing it.

2. Facial Expressions:

- Smile to show approachability and warmth.

- Match your expression to your message—don't smile when delivering serious news.

3. Eye Contact:

- Hold steady eye contact to convey confidence and attentiveness.

Active Listening: The Secret Weapon of Communication

Communication is a two-way street. Active listening ensures the other person feels heard, valued, and understood.

Tips for Active Listening:

- **Give full attention:** Eliminate distractions like your phone or wandering thoughts.

- **Use affirmations:** Nod, smile, or say "I see" to show engagement.

- **Paraphrase:** Summarize what they said to confirm understanding.
  Example: "So, you're saying the timeline is a concern?"

Real-Life Example: The Communication Mastery of Barack Obama

Barack Obama is renowned for his ability to connect with diverse audiences. His speeches are clear, empathetic, and delivered with confidence and authenticity. He uses pauses, varying tones, and relatable language to inspire and engage.

Key Takeaway: Communication is about more than delivering a message; it's about creating a connection.

Strategies for Different Contexts

1. In Professional Settings:

- Speak with confidence and clarity during presentations or meetings.

- Use the "3-Point Rule" to structure your ideas: Introduce the topic, discuss 3 key points, and conclude with a summary.

2. In Conflict:

- Use "I" statements to express your feelings without blaming. *Example: "I feel frustrated when deadlines are missed because it impacts the team's progress."*

- Avoid escalating emotions by staying calm and respectful.

3. In Social Interactions:

- Ask open-ended questions to keep conversations flowing. *Example: "What's the most interesting project you've worked on recently?"*

- Share relatable stories to build rapport.

Exercises to Improve Communication Skills

1. **Mirror Practice:**
   Practice delivering a message in front of a mirror. Pay attention to your tone, body language, and facial expressions.

2. **Record and Review:**

   Record yourself speaking and listen for areas to improve—tone, speed, clarity, or filler words.

3. **Role-Playing:**

   Partner with a friend or colleague to role-play challenging scenarios like giving feedback or handling a disagreement.

4. **The 5-Second Rule:**

   Before responding in a conversation, pause for 5 seconds to collect your thoughts. This reduces impulsive reactions and ensures thoughtful responses.

Common Communication Mistakes to Avoid

1. **Over-Talking:** Dominating the conversation without giving others a chance to speak.

2. **Interrupting:** Cutting someone off shows a lack of respect and patience.

3. **Overusing Jargon:** Using overly technical or complex language can alienate your audience.

4. **Ignoring Nonverbal Cues:** Failing to notice your audience's body language can lead to disengagement.

Quick Tips to Elevate Communication Today

- Start every conversation with a smile—it sets a positive tone.

- Use people's names—it makes them feel valued.

- End with a memorable closing line, such as, "Let me know how I can support you further."

Conclusion

Mastering the art of communication is about more than speaking—it's about connecting. The way you express yourself can inspire trust, foster collaboration, and leave a lasting impression. When you combine clear words, intentional nonverbal cues, and active listening, you become someone people want to engage with.

Ask yourself: *How can I make my next conversation more meaningful?* Start there, and watch how the way people perceive you begins to change.

Chapter 9: Confidence as a Perception Multiplier

Confidence is magnetic. It has the power to amplify how others see your capabilities, leadership, and potential. But confidence isn't about arrogance or pretending to be someone you're not—it's about trusting yourself and projecting that belief outward. In this chapter, we'll explore how to cultivate genuine confidence, why it's crucial to shaping perception, and practical strategies to radiate it in every interaction.

The Role of Confidence in Perception

People often equate confidence with competence. Whether it's fair or not, someone who appears confident is more likely to be trusted, respected, and followed. Confidence acts as a multiplier for your skills, making others believe in your abilities as much as you believe in yourself.

Example: Consider two speakers presenting the same idea. The first mumbles, avoids eye contact, and fidgets nervously. The second speaks clearly, maintains steady eye contact, and stands tall. Even if their content is identical, the second speaker will leave a stronger impression simply because of their confident demeanor.

What Confidence Is (and Isn't)

Confidence isn't about being the loudest person in the room or pretending to know everything. It's about:

- **Believing in your abilities:** Trusting that you have what it takes to handle challenges.

- **Accepting imperfections:** Recognizing that it's okay to make mistakes and learn from them.

- **Projecting self-assurance:** Communicating your belief in yourself through your words, actions, and presence.

It's not:

- Arrogance: Overestimating your abilities or dismissing others.

- Perfectionism: Waiting to feel "ready" before acting.

Why Confidence Matters

1. **Trust Building:** People gravitate toward those who seem self-assured. Confidence signals reliability and competence.

2. **Influence:** Confident individuals are more persuasive because their belief in themselves inspires others to believe in them too.

3. **Resilience:** Confidence helps you bounce back from setbacks, which in turn shapes how others perceive your strength and determination.

How to Cultivate Genuine Confidence

1. Start with Self-Awareness:
Confidence begins with understanding your strengths and weaknesses.

- List your top 3 skills or achievements to remind yourself of your capabilities.

- Identify areas where you feel less confident and make a plan to improve them gradually.

2. Practice Positive Self-Talk:

Your inner dialogue shapes how you feel about yourself. Replace negative thoughts with empowering ones.

- Instead of: "I'm not good enough for this role."

- Say: "I've worked hard to get here, and I'm capable of succeeding."

3. Prepare and Practice:

Confidence grows with preparation. Whether it's a presentation, a meeting, or a social event, knowing your material or role boosts self-assurance.

4. Focus on Body Language:

- Stand tall with your shoulders back—it signals confidence.

- Smile—it makes you approachable and helps you feel at ease.

- Maintain steady eye contact—it conveys trustworthiness.

5. Take Small Risks:

Every success builds confidence. Start with small challenges, like speaking up in a meeting, and gradually tackle bigger ones.

6. Celebrate Progress:

Acknowledge and celebrate your wins, no matter how small. This reinforces your belief in your abilities.

The Power of Acting Confident

Sometimes, confidence follows action. Even if you don't feel fully confident, acting as though you are can change your internal state. This phenomenon, known as "fake it till you make it," works because the brain often follows the body's cues.

Example: If you're nervous before a presentation, try adopting a power pose (e.g., standing tall with hands on your hips) for two minutes. Research shows this can increase feelings of confidence and reduce stress hormones.

Real-Life Example: Serena Williams' Confidence Under Pressure

Serena Williams, one of the greatest tennis players of all time, is a testament to confidence in action. Even in moments of doubt or intense competition, she exudes self-belief through her posture, expressions, and fierce focus. Her ability to project confidence, even when the odds are against her, inspires not only her fans but also her own performance.

Key Takeaway: Confidence isn't about always feeling certain—it's about choosing to project strength and determination in the face of challenges.

How to Appear Confident in Key Situations

1. In Meetings or Presentations:

- Speak clearly and at a steady pace—rushing can signal nervousness.

- Use open gestures to emphasize key points.

- Avoid apologizing unnecessarily.

2. In Conversations:

- Maintain eye contact—it shows engagement and self-assurance.

- Don't be afraid of pauses. They give you time to think and show you're thoughtful.

3. During Conflict:

- Stay calm and composed, even when emotions run high.

- Express your perspective assertively, not aggressively.

Exercises to Build Confidence

1. The Confidence Journal:
Write down three things you did well each day. This practice trains your brain to focus on your strengths.

2. Visualization:
Before a challenging situation, close your eyes and imagine yourself succeeding. Picture the details—your tone, body language, and the positive response from others.

3. Daily Affirmations:
Start your day with affirmations like, "I am capable," or "I deserve success." Over time, these statements reinforce a positive self-image.

Common Confidence Killers (and How to Avoid Them)

1. **Comparing Yourself to Others:**

    - Remember, everyone's journey is different. Focus on your own growth.

2. **Overthinking:**

    - Trust your instincts and avoid second-guessing every decision.

3. **Fear of Failure:**

   o   Embrace failure as a learning opportunity. Even the most successful people have stumbled along the way.

Quick Confidence Boosters to Use Today

- **Stand Tall:** Good posture can instantly make you feel more powerful.

- **Compliment Others:** Focusing on the positive can shift your mindset and make you feel more in control.

- **Dress for Success:** Wear something that makes you feel confident—it sets the tone for the day.

Conclusion

Confidence isn't a trait you're born with—it's a skill you can develop. By building self-awareness, practicing positive habits, and embracing challenges, you can cultivate genuine self-assurance. Confidence not only changes how you see yourself but also how the world sees you.

Ask yourself: *What small step can I take today to feel more confident?* Start there, and watch how your confidence begins to reshape perceptions and open doors.

Chapter 10: Overcoming Negative Labels

At some point in life, we all face labels—descriptions, judgments, or assumptions placed on us by others. Whether it's being seen as "too shy," "not experienced enough," or "difficult to work with," these labels can weigh heavily on how others perceive us and how we see ourselves. The good news is, negative labels aren't permanent. This chapter will show you how to identify, challenge, and overcome these labels to rewrite your narrative.

The Power of Labels

Labels can stick, shaping how others view us and even how we behave. A single negative comment or judgment can overshadow our skills and achievements if left unchecked.

Example: A team member labeled as "difficult" might get excluded from important discussions, even if their ideas are valuable. This cycle reinforces the perception, making it harder for them to break free.

However, labels don't define your worth—they reflect a moment in time, not your entire story.

Why Negative Labels Persist

1. **Confirmation Bias:** Once someone labels you, they tend to notice behaviors that reinforce their belief while ignoring evidence to the contrary.

2. **Lack of Communication:** Misunderstandings or assumptions can create labels that go unchallenged.

3. **Self-Fulfilling Prophecy:** If you internalize a label, you may unconsciously act in ways that validate it.

Real-Life Example: J.K. Rowling and the Label of "Failure"

Before becoming one of the most successful authors in history, J.K. Rowling faced rejection after rejection. She was labeled a "failure" by publishers, society, and even herself. Instead of letting that define her, Rowling used her setbacks as motivation to persevere. Today, she's a global icon whose story inspires millions.

Key Takeaway: Labels are only as powerful as the meaning you assign to them.

Steps to Overcome Negative Labels

1. Identify the Label:
Reflect on how others perceive you and how you perceive yourself.

- What negative labels have been assigned to you?

- Are there recurring patterns or comments?

Example: "People see me as disorganized" or "I'm always called too quiet."

2. Understand the Source:
Labels often stem from a specific incident or misunderstanding. Ask yourself:

- When did this label first appear?

- Is it based on fact, or is it someone else's projection?

3. Challenge the Label:
Ask yourself:

- Is this label accurate, or is it an exaggeration?

- What evidence do I have that contradicts this label?

- Is this label holding me back, or can I use it as a motivator?

4. Reframe the Narrative:
Shift the perception of the label by highlighting its positive side.

- "Being quiet" can be reframed as being thoughtful or a good listener.

- "Too emotional" can become empathetic and passionate.

Example: If labeled as "too inexperienced," focus on your fresh perspective and willingness to learn.

5. Take Action to Redefine Yourself:
Consistent actions can rewrite how others perceive you.

- If labeled as "disorganized," start arriving early, keeping detailed notes, and meeting deadlines consistently.

- If seen as "shy," practice speaking up in small ways, like sharing ideas in meetings or initiating conversations.

6. Communicate Your Transformation:
Don't leave it to others to notice your growth—show them.

- Use phrases like, "I've been working on improving X, and here's how I've progressed."

- Highlight your achievements in subtle ways, such as, "Last week's project really helped me improve my time management skills."

The Role of Feedback in Breaking Labels

Feedback can be a powerful tool for overcoming labels. Seek input from trusted colleagues, friends, or mentors.

- Ask, "What's one thing I could improve on?"

- Follow up: "Do you see any changes in this area?"

This not only helps you grow but also signals to others that you're committed to self-improvement.

Practical Example: Overcoming the "Not a Team Player" Label

Imagine being labeled as "not a team player" due to a misunderstanding or isolated incident.

- **Step 1:** Identify the behavior that led to the label (e.g., preferring to work independently).

- **Step 2:** Reframe the narrative (e.g., highlight how your independence can benefit team efficiency).

- **Step 3:** Take deliberate actions, like volunteering for team projects or offering help to colleagues.

- **Step 4:** Communicate your efforts by sharing team successes and giving credit to others.

Over time, these actions will shift how people perceive you.

Exercises to Break Free from Labels

1. The "Evidence List" Exercise:
Write down every accomplishment, skill, or positive feedback that contradicts a negative label you've been assigned.

- Label: "Disorganized"

- Evidence: "I completed X project on time and organized Y event successfully."

2. Role-Playing:

Practice scenarios where you challenge or reframe labels with a friend.

- Example: "People say I'm too quiet, but I've been using my listening skills to contribute meaningful insights in meetings."

3. The "Future Self" Vision:

Visualize the person you want to become. Write down three actions you can take today to align yourself with that image.

Common Mistakes to Avoid When Dealing with Labels

1. **Defensiveness:** Reacting defensively can reinforce negative perceptions. Stay calm and focus on solutions.

2. **Ignoring Feedback:** While some labels are baseless, others may highlight areas for growth. Be open to constructive criticism.

3. **Expecting Instant Results:** Changing perceptions takes time. Be patient and consistent in your efforts.

Quick Wins to Overcome Labels Today

- Acknowledge a past mistake and share what you've learned from it.

- Volunteer for a task that challenges the negative perception (e.g., leading a project if labeled as "unmotivated").

- Start a conversation with someone who might hold the label against you to clarify or address misunderstandings.

Conclusion

Labels are powerful, but they are not permanent. By identifying the source, challenging the narrative, and taking deliberate action, you can rewrite how others see you. Remember, the only person who defines your worth is you. Use negative labels as fuel to grow, evolve, and reshape your story.

Ask yourself: *What label is holding me back, and how can I take the first step to rewrite it today?*

Chapter 11: The Influence of Appearance and Style

First impressions often begin with what people see. Your appearance and style are powerful tools that shape how others perceive you, often before you even speak a word. While appearance alone doesn't define you, it serves as a visual representation of your personal brand. This chapter explores how to align your appearance with the message you want to send and how small changes can make a big difference in the way people perceive you.

Why Appearance and Style Matter

Research shows that people form impressions of others within the first **seven seconds** of meeting them. These impressions are heavily influenced by visual cues, such as clothing, grooming, and overall presentation. While this may seem superficial, it's rooted in human psychology—appearance serves as an easy way to gauge someone's professionalism, personality, and attention to detail.

Example: Imagine meeting two professionals for the first time. One is neatly dressed, with polished shoes and a well-fitted outfit, while the other wears wrinkled clothes and scuffed shoes. Regardless of their skills or qualifications, your initial perception will likely favor the first person.

What Your Appearance Communicates

Your appearance sends subconscious messages about:

1. **Professionalism:** Are you detail-oriented and reliable?

2. **Confidence:** Do you project self-assurance through your style?

3. **Respect:** Do you respect the occasion, environment, or people you're meeting?

4. **Personality:** Does your style reflect who you are—creative, approachable, or authoritative?

Building an Appearance That Aligns With Your Brand

1. Dress With Intention:
Your clothing should reflect your role, goals, and the context of the situation.

- In professional settings, opt for clean, well-fitted attire that aligns with your industry norms.

- For creative industries, add personal touches, like bold colors or unique accessories, to showcase your individuality.

2. Focus on Grooming:
Good grooming habits signal attention to detail and self-respect.

- Maintain clean and styled hair.

- Ensure nails, skin, and hygiene are well-kept.

- Wear subtle yet pleasant fragrances that leave a positive impression.

3. Invest in Fit Over Fashion:
Clothing doesn't need to be expensive, but it should fit you well. Ill-fitting clothes can make you appear less polished, even if they're trendy or high-quality.

4. Choose Colors Strategically:
Colors evoke emotions and perceptions.

- Neutral colors like navy, black, and gray convey professionalism and authority.

- Bright colors like red and yellow can add energy and confidence.

- Pastels and earth tones project approachability and calmness.

5. Accessorize Thoughtfully:
Accessories, like watches, ties, or jewelry, can elevate your look without being overwhelming. Keep it minimal and purposeful to avoid distractions.

Real-Life Example: Mark Zuckerberg's Simplified Style

Mark Zuckerberg, CEO of Meta, is known for his minimalist wardrobe of gray T-shirts and hoodies. While this might seem casual for a tech billionaire, it's a deliberate choice that aligns with his personal brand of simplicity and efficiency. His consistent style minimizes decision fatigue while maintaining focus on his work.

Key Takeaway: Your style doesn't have to be flashy—it should reflect your values and purpose.

How to Build Your Signature Style

1. Define Your Goals:
Ask yourself: What do I want people to think when they see me?

- Professional? Creative? Approachable?
  Your answer will guide your clothing, grooming, and accessories.

2. Audit Your Wardrobe:
Sort your clothes into categories:

- Items that reflect your personal brand.

- Items that don't fit your current goals or style.
  Donate or retire items that no longer align with your desired image.

3. Start With the Basics:
Invest in wardrobe essentials that can be mixed and matched, such as:

- A tailored blazer.

- Crisp white and light blue shirts.

- Neutral-colored trousers or skirts.

- Comfortable yet professional shoes.

4. Experiment and Evolve:
Don't be afraid to try new styles or accessories. Building your signature look is a process that evolves with your personality and goals.

How to Adapt Your Appearance for Different Contexts

1. Professional Settings:

- Wear attire that aligns with industry norms.

- Err on the side of formality if you're unsure of the dress code.

2. Social Events:

- Choose outfits that balance comfort with style.

- Add a pop of personality, such as bold colors or unique accessories.

3. Virtual Meetings:

- Dress as if you're attending in person—your top half matters most!

- Pay attention to grooming and lighting to appear polished on camera.

Common Appearance Mistakes to Avoid

1. **Ignoring Grooming:** Neglecting basic hygiene or grooming can overshadow even the most expensive outfit.

2. **Overdoing It:** Flashy or excessive accessories can distract from your professionalism.

3. **Wearing Ill-Fitting Clothes:** Baggy or tight clothing can make you appear unprepared or uncomfortable.

4. **Not Dressing for the Occasion:** Being underdressed (or overdressed) can signal a lack of awareness.

Exercises to Upgrade Your Style Today

1. The "Mirror Test":
Before heading out, stand in front of a mirror and ask yourself: "Does this outfit align with how I want to be perceived?"

2. Build a Capsule Wardrobe:
Create a collection of versatile pieces that can be styled for multiple occasions.

3. Get a Trusted Opinion:
Ask a friend or colleague for honest feedback on your style.

4. Experiment With Colors:
Try adding one new color to your wardrobe this week and note how it makes you feel and how others respond.

Quick Style Tips to Elevate Your Appearance Today

- Iron or steam your clothes—it makes an immediate difference.

- Invest in one high-quality accessory, like a watch or bag, that complements most outfits.

- Wear shoes that are polished and clean—they often get noticed first.

- Pay attention to posture—standing tall improves both your appearance and confidence.

Conclusion

Your appearance and style are visual tools that amplify your personal brand. By aligning them with your goals and values, you can create a powerful first impression that reinforces your skills and personality. Remember, the way you present yourself is a reflection of how you want to be perceived.

Ask yourself: *What does my appearance say about me today, and how can I fine-tune it to match the story I want to tell?*

Chapter 12: The Digital You: Perception in the Online World

In today's hyper-connected world, your online presence is as crucial as your in-person interactions. Whether you're aware of it or not, your digital footprint—social media profiles, professional networks, and online activity—shapes how others perceive you. This chapter dives into the importance of curating your online presence, aligning it with your personal brand, and using digital tools to leave a lasting impression.

Why Your Online Presence Matters

With over half the world online, people often form impressions about you based on what they see on your digital profiles before they ever meet you. Recruiters, clients, and even potential collaborators often Google someone before engaging with them. Your online presence can either work for you or against you.

Example: A well-structured LinkedIn profile with professional achievements can boost your credibility, while unfiltered posts on social media might unintentionally damage your reputation.

Key Components of Your Digital Presence

1. Social Media Profiles:
Platforms like LinkedIn, Twitter, Instagram, and Facebook reflect your personal and professional identity. Ensure they align with the image you want to project.

2. Personal Branding on LinkedIn:

- A professional profile photo and compelling headline are non-negotiable.

- Highlight key achievements in your summary and experience sections.

- Post thought leadership content relevant to your field to position yourself as an expert.

3. Online Search Results:
Search your name on Google and evaluate the results. Do they reflect the person you want others to see?

4. Digital Etiquette:
How you interact online—your comments, shares, and tone—plays a huge role in shaping perceptions.

How to Curate Your Digital Footprint

1. Audit Your Current Online Presence:

- Search for your name online and review your social media posts, photos, and tags.

- Remove or hide content that might be perceived as unprofessional or inconsistent with your personal brand.

2. Build a Professional LinkedIn Profile:

- Use a clear, high-quality profile picture.

- Craft a headline that highlights your expertise (e.g., "Data-Driven Marketing Strategist | Building Growth-Focused Campaigns").

- Write a summary that tells your story, emphasizing your strengths and values.

- Regularly update your skills, achievements, and certifications.

3. Align Content With Your Goals:

- Post content that reflects your values, expertise, and interests.

- Avoid controversial topics unless they align with your brand and are communicated thoughtfully.

4. Separate Personal and Professional:

- Consider creating separate accounts for personal and professional use on platforms like Twitter or Instagram.

- Use privacy settings wisely to control who sees your personal posts.

5. Be Consistent Across Platforms:

- Ensure your photo, tone, and bio are aligned across all platforms. Inconsistencies can confuse people about your identity or credibility.

The Power of Thought Leadership Online

Positioning yourself as a thought leader online can significantly boost how others perceive you. Share valuable insights, engage in industry discussions, and demonstrate your expertise.

Example:

- Post blogs or articles on LinkedIn showcasing your knowledge.

- Participate in relevant Twitter threads or LinkedIn groups to build visibility and credibility.

Real-Life Example: Gary Vaynerchuk's Digital Presence

Gary Vaynerchuk is a master of leveraging his digital presence to shape perceptions. Through consistent, high-quality content on platforms like YouTube, LinkedIn, and Instagram, he has positioned himself as a marketing expert and thought leader. His tone, style, and messages are consistent, making his brand recognizable and impactful.

Key Takeaway: Consistency and value-driven content are critical for building a strong online identity.

Avoiding Digital Pitfalls

1. Oversharing:
Revealing too much personal information can dilute your professional image.

2. Negativity:
Frequent complaints, arguments, or aggressive comments can harm your reputation.

3. Inactivity:
An outdated or inactive profile can signal a lack of engagement or relevance.

4. Unprofessional Photos or Posts:
Images or posts that don't align with your personal brand can leave a lasting negative impression.

How to Leverage Digital Tools

1. Personal Website:
Create a simple website showcasing your skills, portfolio, and contact information. Platforms like Wix or WordPress make it easy to build one.

2. Online Portfolios:

For creative professionals, platforms like Behance or Dribbble allow you to display your work and attract opportunities.

3. Social Media Scheduling Tools:

Use tools like Buffer or Hootsuite to plan and maintain a consistent posting schedule.

4. Analytics:

Track your engagement on platforms like LinkedIn to understand what content resonates with your audience.

Practical Steps to Start Today

1. Update Your LinkedIn Profile:

Spend 20 minutes refining your headline, summary, and recent achievements.

2. Google Yourself:

Search your name online and identify content to clean up or improve.

3. Plan Your Content Calendar:

Draft 3-5 posts you can share over the next month, such as an article, an industry insight, or a personal success story.

4. Engage Thoughtfully:

Comment on 3-5 posts from people in your network to start building meaningful connections.

Quick Wins for a Polished Digital Presence

- Use the same professional photo across all platforms for consistency.

- Add a professional email signature with links to your LinkedIn or website.

- Regularly update your achievements and skills on LinkedIn.

- Respond promptly and politely to messages or comments.

Conclusion

Your online presence is a powerful extension of your personal brand. By curating and maintaining it thoughtfully, you can amplify your strengths, build trust, and create opportunities. Remember, in the digital age, people will form opinions about you long before meeting you in person. Make sure your online persona reflects the best version of yourself.

Ask yourself: *What does my digital presence say about me today, and how can I refine it to align with my goals?*

Chapter 13: The Role of Habits in Shaping Perception

Habits are the invisible architects of your life. They shape not only your behavior but also how others perceive you over time. Consistently showing up in a certain way—whether as reliable, confident, or driven—builds a strong personal brand and reinforces the way people see you. This chapter explores how to develop positive habits that enhance your reputation and how to break habits that might be holding you back.

Why Habits Matter in Perception

While one-off actions can create an impression, habits are what solidify perceptions. They create a pattern of behavior that others notice and remember. For example:

- Someone who consistently meets deadlines will be seen as dependable.

- Someone who is always late might be labeled as unreliable.

Example: Imagine a team member who always volunteers for tough assignments and follows through. Over time, they'll be seen as proactive and trustworthy, even without explicitly stating those qualities.

The Science of Habits and Perception

Habits are driven by a feedback loop: **Cue → Routine → Reward.** Over time, these loops become automatic, defining how you show up in the world. By consciously tweaking these loops, you can align your habits with the image you want to project.

Example of a Habit Loop:

- **Cue:** You get an email notification.

- **Routine:** You respond promptly.

- **Reward:** You're seen as responsive and engaged.

How to Build Positive Habits That Shape Perception

1. Start Small but Be Consistent:
Big changes don't happen overnight. Focus on small, consistent actions that align with the way you want to be perceived.

- If you want to be seen as reliable, start by always being 5 minutes early to meetings.

- If you want to be seen as organized, end each day by tidying your workspace.

2. Align Habits With Your Desired Image:
Ask yourself:

- What qualities do I want people to associate with me?

- What daily habits would reinforce those qualities?

Example: If you want to be seen as approachable, develop the habit of greeting colleagues with a warm smile or checking in with team members regularly.

3. Use Accountability:
Share your goals with a trusted friend or colleague. Their feedback and encouragement will help reinforce your habits and keep you on track.

4. Replace Negative Habits With Positive Ones:
It's easier to replace a habit than to eliminate it entirely. For example:

- Replace procrastination with a habit of starting your day by tackling one small, high-priority task.

Breaking Habits That Hurt Your Perception

Negative habits, even small ones, can undermine how others see you.

1. Identify Your Negative Habits:
Reflect on behaviors that might be holding you back.

- Do you frequently interrupt others during conversations?

- Are you often late or miss deadlines?

2. Understand the Root Cause:
Habits often stem from specific triggers.

- Example: If you interrupt others, is it because you're excited or afraid you'll forget your point?

3. Replace, Don't Erase:
Swap the negative habit for a positive one.

- Instead of interrupting, practice active listening and take notes to remember your point.

4. Track Your Progress:
Keep a journal or checklist to monitor your efforts in breaking a bad habit.

Real-Life Example: Warren Buffett's Discipline

Warren Buffett is renowned for his disciplined habits, such as reading for hours each day to deepen his knowledge. This consistency has shaped his reputation as one of the most thoughtful and strategic investors of all time.

Key Takeaway: Small, consistent habits create lasting impressions and reinforce how people perceive your expertise and character.

Habits That Enhance Positive Perception

1. **Punctuality:**

   o   Always being on time signals reliability and respect for others' time.

2. **Follow-Through:**

   o   Delivering on promises builds trust and credibility.

3. **Proactive Communication:**

   o   Keeping people informed, even about small updates, shows engagement and responsibility.

4. **Continuous Learning:**

   o   Regularly seeking out new knowledge or skills demonstrates ambition and adaptability.

5. **Gratitude:**

   o   Saying "thank you" and acknowledging others' efforts fosters goodwill and respect.

Daily Habits to Try Today

1. **The 5-Minute Review:**
   At the end of each day, review your actions and interactions. Ask yourself: "Did my actions today align with how I want to be perceived?"

2. **Morning Focus:**

   Start each day by identifying one key action that will enhance how others see you.

3. **The Power of the Pause:**

   Before responding in conversations or emails, take a moment to consider your tone and message.

4. **Consistent Self-Reflection:**

   Dedicate 10 minutes weekly to reflect on your habits and identify areas for improvement.

Common Pitfalls When Building Habits

1. **Trying to Change Too Much at Once:**

   Focus on one or two habits at a time to avoid feeling overwhelmed.

2. **Expecting Immediate Results:**

   Habits take time to form. Be patient and consistent.

3. **Ignoring Feedback:**

   Listen to how others respond to your behavior—it's a valuable source of insight into how your habits are shaping perception.

4. **Perfectionism:**

   Don't let small slip-ups derail your progress. The goal is improvement, not perfection.

Quick Wins to Improve Perception Through Habits

- **Respond promptly to emails or messages.** This builds trust and shows engagement.

- **End meetings with a clear summary of your contributions.** It reinforces your value.

- **Adopt the habit of asking others how you can support them.** It shows teamwork and empathy.

- **Practice consistent follow-ups.** After a meeting or project, checking in demonstrates reliability and attention to detail.

Conclusion

Habits are the building blocks of your personal brand. By cultivating positive, consistent habits and replacing negative ones, you can shape how others see you in a lasting, meaningful way. The key is to start small, stay consistent, and align your habits with the person you want to become.

Ask yourself: *What one habit can I start today to make a positive shift in how I'm perceived?* Let that small step be the beginning of a powerful transformation.

Chapter 14: Real-Time Strategies for Shaping Perception

Shaping perception isn't always about long-term habits or major overhauls; sometimes, it's about what you do in the moment. Real-time strategies can help you leave the right impression in meetings, conversations, or unplanned interactions. In this chapter, we'll explore techniques to make an immediate impact, whether you're meeting someone for the first time, handling a tough situation, or navigating social dynamics.

Why Real-Time Perception Matters

Every interaction is an opportunity to shape how others see you. The way you handle yourself in real-time situations—especially when the stakes are high—can solidify a positive perception or undo months of effort.

Example: Imagine being in a meeting where someone challenges your idea. If you respond calmly and thoughtfully, you'll be seen as composed and confident. If you become defensive or flustered, it may raise doubts about your professionalism.

Key Principles of Real-Time Perception Management

1. Stay Present and Engaged:
People notice when you're distracted or disengaged. Focus entirely on the conversation or situation at hand.

2. Manage Your Emotions:
Your ability to stay composed under pressure speaks volumes about

your character. Even in challenging moments, maintain control over your tone and body language.

3. Adapt Quickly:

Real-time situations often require flexibility. Adjusting your approach based on the audience or environment shows that you're adaptable and in tune with others' needs.

Practical Real-Time Strategies

1. The 3-Second Pause:

Before reacting, pause for three seconds to gather your thoughts. This prevents impulsive responses and ensures you communicate intentionally.

- Use this in heated discussions to avoid saying something you might regret.

2. Active Listening:

Show that you're fully engaged by:

- Maintaining eye contact.

- Nodding or offering affirmations like "I see" or "That's a good point."

- Paraphrasing key points to confirm understanding.

3. Speak With Clarity:

In real-time situations, how you say something matters as much as what you say.

- Use short, clear sentences.

- Avoid filler words like "um" or "you know."

- Emphasize key points with a calm, steady tone.

4. Use Nonverbal Cues to Reinforce Confidence:

- Sit or stand tall to convey authority.

- Use open gestures to emphasize points without overdoing it.

- Keep a relaxed facial expression to appear approachable.

5. Handle Criticism Gracefully:
When faced with criticism or feedback:

- Thank the person for their perspective.

- Avoid defensiveness—seek to understand their point of view.

- Respond with a solution or plan for improvement, showing accountability.

Real-Life Example: Indra Nooyi's Listening Strategy

As the former CEO of PepsiCo, Indra Nooyi was known for her ability to listen deeply and respond thoughtfully in meetings. She once shared that when people came to her with ideas, she would take detailed notes to show her attentiveness and respect for their input. This simple real-time strategy helped her build trust and foster collaboration within her team.

Key Takeaway: Real-time actions, like active listening, can leave a lasting positive impression.

Strategies for Specific Scenarios

1. Meeting Someone New:

- Smile warmly and offer a firm handshake.

- Introduce yourself clearly with confidence.

- Ask open-ended questions to show genuine interest in the other person.

2. Speaking in Meetings:

- Begin with a concise point or insight to capture attention.

- Back up your ideas with data or examples to demonstrate credibility.

- Summarize your points at the end to reinforce your message.

3. Handling Tough Questions:

- Stay calm and take a moment to think before answering.

- Use phrases like "That's a great question. Here's how I would approach it…"

- If you don't know the answer, say, "Let me get back to you with more information on that."

4. Navigating Social Settings:

- Be mindful of group dynamics—don't dominate the conversation, but don't fade into the background either.

- Look for opportunities to connect with quieter individuals— they'll appreciate the effort.

- Share relatable stories or insights to engage others.

Real-Time Perception Builders

1. Compliment With Specificity:
Instead of generic compliments, focus on specifics.

- Example: "Your presentation was insightful, especially the section on market trends—it really stood out."

2. Use Names Frequently:
People respond positively when you use their name in conversations—it shows attentiveness and respect.

3. Acknowledge Others' Contributions:
When someone shares an idea or helps with a task, acknowledge it publicly.

- Example: "I appreciate the effort Priya put into organizing this— it made a huge difference."

4. End With a Strong Closing Statement:
Whether it's a meeting or casual interaction, leave people with a memorable takeaway.

- Example: "It's been great discussing this with you—I'm looking forward to collaborating further."

Common Real-Time Mistakes to Avoid

1. **Interrupting:** Cutting someone off makes you seem impatient or disrespectful. Wait for them to finish speaking.

2. **Overreacting:** Avoid emotional outbursts, even in stressful situations. Take a breath and respond calmly.

3. **Over-Talking:** Saying too much can dilute your message. Focus on making concise, impactful points.

4. **Failing to Read the Room:** Pay attention to others' body language and tone—adjust your approach if needed.

Exercises to Improve Real-Time Perception

1. The "5-Second Rule" in Conversations:
Before responding, pause for five seconds to collect your thoughts and ensure your response is intentional.

2. Practice Active Listening Daily:
Choose one conversation each day where you focus solely on listening. Avoid interrupting and summarize what the other person said at the end.

3. Simulate Scenarios:
Role-play real-time situations with a friend or mentor, such as handling a tough question or introducing yourself at a networking event.

Quick Wins to Apply in Real-Time Today

- Maintain eye contact when speaking and listening—it builds trust.

- Replace "I think" with "I believe" to sound more confident.

- Summarize key points before ending a conversation to reinforce clarity.

- Start conversations with a compliment or warm greeting to set a positive tone.

Conclusion

In real-time situations, every word, gesture, and response contributes to how others perceive you. By staying composed, listening actively, and responding intentionally, you can turn every interaction into an opportunity to reinforce your personal brand.

Ask yourself: *How can I show up in my next interaction to leave a lasting positive impression?* Every moment is a chance to shape the way others see you—make it count.

Chapter 15: Your Perception Transformation Blueprint

Changing how others perceive you doesn't happen overnight—it's a journey of intentional action, self-awareness, and consistent effort. This final chapter provides a step-by-step blueprint to help you apply the concepts and strategies from the previous chapters to transform your perception and achieve the success you desire.

Step 1: Define Your Desired Perception

Before you can change how others see you, you need to clearly define how you want to be perceived.

Ask Yourself:

- What qualities do I want people to associate with me? (e.g., confident, trustworthy, approachable, knowledgeable)

- What roles or situations am I trying to improve my perception in? (e.g., at work, with clients, in social settings)

Write Your Perception Statement:
This is a one-sentence declaration of how you want to be perceived.
Example: "I want to be seen as a confident and reliable leader who inspires trust and delivers results."

Step 2: Audit Your Current Perception

Understand where you stand now by seeking honest feedback and reflecting on your actions.

Gather Feedback:

- Ask colleagues, friends, or mentors: "What's one thing I do well?" and "What's one area where I could improve?"

- Review past interactions—how have others responded to you?

Identify Gaps:

Compare your desired perception with your current reputation. Where are the disconnects?

Step 3: Build a Strategy for Alignment

Once you know where you stand and where you want to go, create a plan to bridge the gap.

Focus Areas:

- **Appearance and Style:** Align your outward presentation with your desired image.

- **Communication:** Practice clarity, confidence, and empathy in conversations.

- **Habits:** Cultivate consistent behaviors that reinforce your brand.

Example: If you want to be seen as a confident communicator, focus on improving your public speaking skills and reducing filler words.

Step 4: Leverage Small Wins for Momentum

Start with small, consistent changes to build momentum and reinforce new habits.

Quick Wins:

- Arrive on time (or early) to every meeting to signal reliability.

- Maintain eye contact and a strong posture during conversations.

- Replace negative self-talk with positive affirmations.

- Use people's names in conversations to build rapport.

Step 5: Track Your Progress

Perception transformation requires regular reflection and adjustment.

Keep a Perception Journal:

- At the end of each week, ask yourself:

    o   Did my actions align with how I want to be perceived?

    o   What went well?

    o   What can I improve?

Review Feedback:

- Regularly check in with trusted peers or mentors for feedback on your progress.

Step 6: Handle Setbacks Gracefully

No transformation journey is without challenges. Mistakes happen, but how you handle them can shape perceptions even more.

Tips for Handling Setbacks:

- **Own It:** If you make a mistake, acknowledge it quickly and sincerely.
  Example: "I realize I missed the deadline—I take full responsibility and will ensure it doesn't happen again."

- **Focus on Solutions:** Instead of dwelling on the mistake, shift the focus to how you'll resolve it.

- **Learn and Move On:** Treat every setback as an opportunity for growth.

Step 7: Reinforce Your Brand Consistently

Consistency is key to shaping and maintaining your desired perception. Over time, repeated actions build trust and solidify your personal brand.

Be Predictable in Positive Ways:

- Always follow through on commitments.

- Respond to challenges with calmness and confidence.

- Stay aligned with your core values, even in tough situations.

Example Blueprint for Transformation

Goal: Be perceived as a confident and approachable leader.

Actions:

1. Start every meeting by greeting everyone warmly and using their names.

2. Speak with clarity and avoid filler words during presentations.

3. Offer constructive feedback to team members, showing empathy and encouragement.

4. Dress in a polished, professional style that reflects your role.

5. Reflect weekly on your progress and seek feedback from trusted peers.

Common Pitfalls to Avoid

1. **Inconsistency:** Sending mixed signals through behavior, appearance, or communication can confuse others.

2. **Impatience:** Transforming perception takes time. Avoid rushing the process—focus on gradual progress.

3. **Overcompensating:** Avoid trying too hard to prove yourself, which can come across as inauthentic.

4. **Ignoring Feedback:** Constructive criticism is a gift—use it to refine your actions.

Your Perception Checklist

1. **Self-Awareness:**

    o   Am I clear on how I want to be perceived?

    o   Do I understand my strengths and areas for growth?

2. **Alignment:**

    o   Does my appearance, communication, and behavior reflect my desired image?

3. **Consistency:**

    o   Am I showing up the same way in all interactions, across both professional and personal settings?

4. **Reflection:**

- o Am I regularly reviewing my progress and adjusting as needed?

5. **Authenticity:**

- o Am I staying true to myself while improving how others see me?

Conclusion: Your New Chapter Starts Now

Transforming how others perceive you is one of the most empowering journeys you can embark on. By taking small, intentional steps every day, you can align your actions with the story you want to tell. Remember, perception is shaped by what you do consistently, not what you do occasionally.

Ask yourself: *What is the first step I can take today to become the person I want others to see?* The journey begins now—one action, one habit, one interaction at a time.

Your transformation isn't just possible—it's inevitable when you take control of your narrative.

Epilogue

Perception is a powerful tool—one that shapes opportunities, influences relationships, and defines success. Over the course of this book, we've explored the secrets of influence, confidence, and charisma, breaking them down into practical, actionable steps. But knowledge alone isn't enough. **The real transformation begins when you apply what you've learned.**

By now, you understand that the way people perceive you isn't set in stone. **It can be shaped, refined, and elevated.** You have the ability to project confidence, communicate with authority, and create a lasting impact in every interaction. Whether in your personal life, your career, or your social circles, **your presence matters—and you have control over how it is experienced by others.**

But this journey doesn't end here. Mastering perception is an ongoing process—one that evolves as you grow. Continue refining your skills, experimenting with different strategies, and stepping outside your comfort zone. Observe the way people respond to you, take feedback constructively, and keep pushing yourself toward **the best version of you**.

And most importantly, remember this: **authenticity is the foundation of true influence**. The goal is not to manipulate or deceive, but to present yourself **intentionally and effectively** in a way that aligns with your goals and values. Confidence, charisma, and influence are not about pretending to be someone you're not—they are about becoming more of who you were meant to be.

So, as you close this book, step forward with purpose. **Own your presence. Shape your perception. Influence your world.**

The power is in your hands.

[Tom Crowe]